Ladybug

Horned Beetle

Stinkbug

Stick Bug

This book is dedicated to my son, Jason, because of his appreciation for the small things in life, including bugs.

這本書要獻給我的兒子——Jason，因為他總能去欣賞生活中的微小事物，包括小蟲子。

# Stilt's Stick Problem

## 史提的大麻煩

Stilt the stick bug likes to *play tricks on his friends.
He makes his body *stiff so he looks like a *branch.
Soon, Fleet the fly *lands on a leaf.

*為生字，請參照生字表

"Stilt?" Fleet calls. "Where are you?"

"Right here!"

Stilt jumps up beside her.

Fleet *grabs a leaf so she doesn't fall.

4

"Ha ha! You almost *fell for my stick trick!"
Stilt cries.

"It's not a stick trick. It's a stick PROBLEM!"
Fleet says angrily. She flies away.

6

Lily the ladybug lands on a leaf to eat lunch.

Stilt moves behind her and makes his body stiff.

He looks so much like a stick that Lily walks along his back.

Suddenly Stilt *shakes his body.

"What's happening?" Lily cries. She flies to another branch.

Lily is *scared. Someone is *playing a joke, but she doesn't see anyone.

11

"W-who's there?"

"It's my stick trick," Stilt says.

"Your stick trick is not funny. It's a stick PROBLEM,"
Lily says angrily. She flies away.

Stilt doesn't listen to Lily. He *looks for someone else to trick. He sees a big, dark *shadow behind the leaf.

"Someone is behind that leaf. I'll try my stick trick on it."

Stilt *leans against the leaf, making his body stiff. "Just what I need to finish my *sunshade," Blister the horned beetle cries.

He grabs Stilt in his strong *jaws and uses him to *prop up the leaf. Stilt tries to call out, but the leaf blocks his mouth. He can't talk!

"Now for a good rest in the shade," Blister says.

As he *relaxes, he sees Fleet and Lily on another leaf.

"Come share my sunshade!" He calls.

"This is a good idea," Lily says.

"I feel something moving on my back,"
Fleet calls in *fear.
Fleet, Lily and Blister look up.
"Oh, no!" Lily cries. "Look, Blister!"

22

"Stilt, is that you?" Blister cries out in surprise.
He *lifts Stilt free of the sunshade.

24

"I thought you were a stick!" Blister cries.

"I thought you wanted to look like a stick," Fleet says.

"I was playing my stick trick," Stilt says. "But I guess it was a stick problem for me!"

They all laugh.

# 生字表

stick [stɪk] n. 樹枝，枝條

*p.3*

play tricks on　惡作劇，戲弄

stiff [stɪf] adj. 僵直的，僵硬的

branch [bræntʃ] n. 樹枝

land [lænd] v. 降落

*p.4*

grab [græb] v. 抓取

*p.6*

fall for　上當，被欺騙

*p.10*

shake [ʃek] v. 搖動，抖動

*p.11*

scared [skɛrd] adj. 害怕的

28

n.=名<sub>ㄇㄧㄥ</sub>詞<sub>ㄘ</sub>，adj.=形<sub>ㄒㄧㄥ</sub>容<sub>ㄖㄨㄥ</sub>詞<sub>ㄘ</sub>，v.=動<sub>ㄉㄨㄥ</sub>詞<sub>ㄘ</sub>

# 史提的大麻煩

竹節蟲史提喜歡捉弄他的朋友。
他讓身體僵直不動，這樣一來，
他看起來就像根樹枝。沒過多
久，蒼蠅飛麗飛到一片葉子上。
飛麗大喊:「史提，你在哪裡?」
「在這裡!」
史提從飛麗身旁跳了出來。飛麗
趕緊抓住一片葉子，免得跌下去。
史提大叫:「哈哈！妳差點被我的
『樹枝把戲』騙倒了!」

飛麗很生氣的說:「這才不是什麼把戲，這是麻煩!」說完她就飛走了。

瓢蟲莉莉也飛到一片葉子上吃午餐。史提走到她的背後，然後挺直著身子不動。他看起來實在太像樹枝了，所以莉莉竟然從他的背上走過去。突然間，史提晃了晃自己的身體。

莉莉大喊:「發生什麼事了?」說完趕緊飛到另一根樹枝上。

她嚇壞了。有人在惡作劇，但是她卻連個

影子都沒看到。

「誰……誰在那裡?」

史提這時才出聲說:「是我的『樹枝把戲』啦!」

莉莉生氣的說:「你的『樹枝把戲』一點都不好玩,它是麻煩!」說完她就飛走了。

史提並沒有把莉莉的話聽進去,繼續去找其他的人來惡作劇。他看到葉子後面有個大大的、黑色

的影子。

「葉子後面有個人耶！讓我再來試試我的『樹枝把戲』吧！」

史提靠在葉子上，身體保持僵直不動。

鍬形蟲小布喊著:「這正好可以拿來做我的遮陽篷呢！」

他用他強壯的大顎夾住史提，並拿他來撐住葉子。史提試著要大叫，但葉子卻堵住他的嘴，讓他沒辦法說話。

小布說:「現在終於可以在陰涼的地方好好

休息啦！」

當他正在休息時，他看到飛麗和莉莉在另一片葉子上。

他大喊：「一起來乘涼吧！」

莉莉說：「好主意！」

飛麗害怕的大叫：「我覺得有東西在我的背後動耶！」

飛麗、莉莉和小布同時抬頭看。

莉莉大叫：「喔，不！小布，快看！」

小布驚訝的喊著：「史提，是你嗎?」

他把史提從遮陽篷上放了下來。

小布大叫：「我還以為你是根樹枝呢！」

飛麗說：「我以為你希望自己看起來像根樹枝。」

史提說：「我只是在玩我的『樹枝把戲』，

但沒想到這會變成我的麻煩！」

大家都笑了。

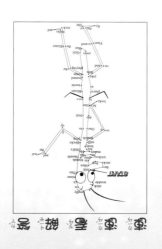

# Connect the Dots

## 連連看

請先閱讀下面的故事，再依照文字的順序把每個點連起來，最後將會出現一個意想不到的圖案。

Stilt the stick bug likes to play tricks on his friends. He makes his body stiff so he looks like a branch. One day he plays a joke on Fleet the fly. She is scared and flies away. But Stilt keeps playing the trick and tricks Blister the horned beetle. Blister uses Stilt to prop up the leaf and it blocks Stilt's mouth. This time it is really a stick problem.

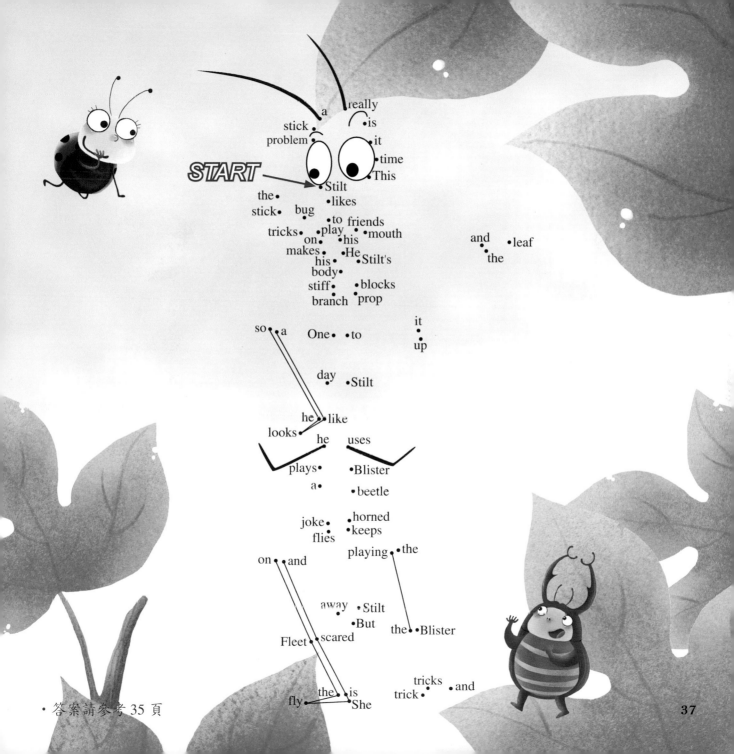

START

# 擬ㄋㄧˊ態ㄊㄞˋ高ㄍㄠ手ㄕㄡˇ
## 竹ㄓㄨˊ節ㄐㄧㄝˊ蟲ㄔㄨㄥˊ

Stick Bug
Stick Insect

「竹ㄓㄨˊ節ㄐㄧㄝˊ蟲ㄔㄨㄥˊ」這ㄓㄜˋ個ㄍㄜˋ名ㄇㄧㄥˊ字ㄗˋ的ㄉㄜ由ㄧㄡˊ來ㄌㄞˊ，是ㄕˋ因ㄧㄣ為ㄨㄟˋ牠ㄊㄚ們ㄇㄣ的ㄉㄜ身ㄕㄣ體ㄊㄧˇ一ㄧˋ節ㄐㄧㄝˊ一ㄧˋ節ㄐㄧㄝˊ的ㄉㄜ類ㄌㄟˋ似ㄙˋ竹ㄓㄨˊ子ㄗ。牠ㄊㄚ們ㄇㄣ的ㄉㄜ身ㄕㄣ體ㄊㄧˇ長ㄔㄤˊ度ㄉㄨˋ通ㄊㄨㄥ常ㄔㄤˊ在ㄗㄞˋ一ㄧ到ㄉㄠˋ十ㄕˊ三ㄙㄢ公ㄍㄨㄥ分ㄈㄣ之ㄓ間ㄐㄧㄢ，最ㄗㄨㄟˋ長ㄔㄤˊ可ㄎㄜˇ達ㄉㄚˊ三ㄙㄢ十ㄕˊ幾ㄐㄧˇ公ㄍㄨㄥ分ㄈㄣ，是ㄕˋ身ㄕㄣ體ㄊㄧˇ最ㄗㄨㄟˋ長ㄔㄤˊ的ㄉㄜ昆ㄎㄨㄣ蟲ㄔㄨㄥˊ。竹ㄓㄨˊ節ㄐㄧㄝˊ蟲ㄔㄨㄥˊ的ㄉㄜ身ㄕㄣ體ㄊㄧˇ顏ㄧㄢˊ色ㄙㄜˋ主ㄓㄨˇ要ㄧㄠˋ為ㄨㄟˊ綠ㄌㄩˋ色ㄙㄜˋ或ㄏㄨㄛˋ褐ㄏㄜˋ色ㄙㄜˋ，頭ㄊㄡˊ很ㄏㄣˇ小ㄒㄧㄠˇ，身ㄕㄣ體ㄊㄧˇ跟ㄍㄣ腳ㄐㄧㄠˇ都ㄉㄡ非ㄈㄟ常ㄔㄤˊ細ㄒㄧˋ長ㄔㄤˊ，就ㄐㄧㄡˋ像ㄒㄧㄤˋ樹ㄕㄨˋ枝ㄓ一ㄧˊ樣ㄧㄤˋ；當ㄉㄤ牠ㄊㄚ們ㄇㄣ一ㄧˋ動ㄉㄨㄥˋ也ㄧㄝˇ不ㄅㄨˋ動ㄉㄨㄥˋ的ㄉㄜ停ㄊㄧㄥˊ在ㄗㄞˋ樹ㄕㄨˋ上ㄕㄤˋ，模ㄇㄛˊ擬ㄋㄧˇ成ㄔㄥˊ樹ㄕㄨˋ枝ㄓ的ㄉㄜ樣ㄧㄤˋ子ㄗ時ㄕˊ，敵ㄉㄧˊ人ㄖㄣˊ幾ㄐㄧ乎ㄏㄨ無ㄨˊ法ㄈㄚˇ分ㄈㄣ辨ㄅㄧㄢˋ出ㄔㄨ來ㄌㄞˊ，這ㄓㄜˋ就ㄐㄧㄡˋ是ㄕˋ牠ㄊㄚ們ㄇㄣ「擬ㄋㄧˊ態ㄊㄞˋ」的ㄉㄜ本ㄅㄣˇ領ㄌㄧㄥˇ。而ㄦˊ牠ㄊㄚ們ㄇㄣ就ㄐㄧㄡˋ是ㄕˋ

靠著這種特性來保護自己，使天敵不容易發現牠們。此外，竹節蟲的身體也會隨著環境變化而改變顏色，例如氣溫或光線明暗都會影響牠們，這也是牠們另一種自我防衛的方式。

其他也會擬態的昆蟲：

枯葉蝶：外形像一片枯葉，藉此讓敵人認不出來。

螳螂：模仿葉片，使昆蟲誤認牠們為葉子而接近，最後再把牠們當作大餐享用。

鹿蛾：外型與攻擊性很強的黃蜂相似，藉此保護自己，免受攻擊。

# 關於作者

Kriss Erickson has been a freelance writer since 1981. She has published in the United States and in Australia and has over 300 published works. Kriss earned a Master's degree in Counseling in 2003 and holds a Master's level certificate of Spiritual Direction. She lives with her husband and son on a 3/4 acre wetland where she has created extensive gardens. Kriss is also a freelance artist in colored pencil and acrylic. She enjoys singing blues and contemporary music at local coffee shops.

Kriss Erickson 從 1981 年開始了自由作家的生活。她陸續在美國和澳洲發表著作，至今出版過的作品已超過 300 本。Kriss 在 2003 年取得心理諮商碩士的學位，並且擁有靈修指導碩士程度的結業證書。她和丈夫以及兒子住在四分之三英畝的濕地上，還在那裡打造了一個廣闊的花園。Kriss 同時也是一位自由藝術家，擅長使用色鉛筆和壓克力顏料來畫畫，而在當地的咖啡店哼唱藍調和現代音樂則是她的樂趣。

# 關於繪者

陽光，綠蔭，
花和青草味，
樹影和月光，蛙鳴。
童年的盛夏。

一個透明的玻璃瓶，瓶口用橡皮筋箍著紙蓋，上面扎有幾個氣孔，將裡面裝滿大大小小的、知名的或是不知名的蟲兒，然後安靜而好奇的看上好長一陣子，這是整個季節裡最興趣盎然的事情之一了。許多歲以後，複雜、莫名的東西多起來，心中不再有那個帶紙蓋的瓶子，不再關心、甚至不再靜心聆聽周圍的一切。

身為卡圖工作室的一份子，畫畫、做書，我們努力為孩子們製造著快樂，同樣也為自己尋找單純和美好。

# 親親自然 成就英語悅讀

台北市外語啟蒙教學發展學會理事長　　李宗玥

　　「故事」是每個孩子的夢工廠，成就孩子的豐富幻想，讓孩子的想像力無限伸展與飛翔，每個故事都在架構成長的快樂回憶，細數故事的數目，如同細數快樂。

　　「自然世界」是兒童生活經驗中，最真實與迷人的經驗。不起眼的毛毛蟲為什麼會變成一隻漂漂亮亮的蝴蝶？自然世界裡充滿了讓孩子忍不住驚喜的讚嘆，如同作者的孩子，琢磨於生活中的微小事物，一隻小蟲子也能成就一個大驚奇，從孩子的眼裡視察自然，會發現自然世界本身就是一個故事屋。

　　「語言」是迎向世界最萬能的鑰匙，它開啟每一扇快樂夢想的門；而每一扇門後，有著世界各個角落裡孩子的喜悅與幻想。有了語言的鑰匙，才有機會透視世界更多的快樂夢想，才有機會了解故事裡的昆蟲們，是如何相處互動的。

三民書局的「我的昆蟲朋友」系列，用「語言」的骨架，串連了「故事」與「自然世界」，搭起孩子閱讀的興趣與動機，讓「語言」(language) 與「知識」(knowledge) 不再毫無交集、枯燥乏味。就是這樣的書，會讓我們和孩子都感動。任何一種有目的的學習，在學習歷程中，都會有高低潮，我相信藉著「我的昆蟲朋友」系列中有趣的自然故事與好玩的學習活動，必然能逐步架構語言的樂趣與能力。

　　語言的學習，早就應擺脫制式語言文法架構，而走入孩子的真實生活裡。如果您也有同樣的想法，相信在「昆蟲朋友」的「自然世界」中，必能滿足您對孩子語言發展的夢想與期盼。

FUN心讀雙語叢書

# BUG BUDDIES SERIES 我的昆蟲朋友系列

具基礎英文閱讀能力者（國小 4～6 年級適讀）

　　我有幾個昆蟲好朋友，各個都有自己奇怪的特性，讓他們有點煩惱；可是這樣的不同，卻帶給他們意想不到的驚奇與結果！

「我的昆蟲朋友」共有五個：

1. Bumpy's Crazy Tail　　邦皮的瘋狂尾巴
2. Fleet's Sticky Feet　　飛麗的黏腳丫
3. Stilt's Stick Problem　史提的大麻煩
4. Macy's Strange Snacks　莓西的怪點心
5. Stinky's Funny Scent　丁奇的怪味道

國家圖書館出版品預行編目資料

Stilt's Stick Problem:史提的大麻煩 / Kriss Erickson著;卡圖工作室繪;本局編輯部譯.－－初版一刷.－－臺北市：三民，2006
　　面；　　公分.－－(Fun心讀雙語叢書.我的昆蟲朋友系列)
中英對照
ISBN 957－14－4592－4　　(精裝)
1.英國語言－讀本
523.38　　　　　　　　　　　　　95014822

© **Stilt's Stick Problem**
　　──史提的大麻煩

著作人　Kriss Erickson
繪　者　卡圖工作室
譯　者　本局編輯部
發行人　劉振強
著作財
產權人　三民書局股份有限公司
　　　　臺北市復興北路386號
發行所　三民書局股份有限公司
　　　　地址／臺北市復興北路386號
　　　　電話／(02)25006600
　　　　郵撥／0009998－5
印刷所　三民書局股份有限公司
門市部　復北店／臺北市復興北路386號
　　　　重南店／臺北市重慶南路一段61號
初版一刷　2006年8月
編　號　S 806751
定　價　新臺幣參佰元整
行政院新聞局登記證局版臺業字第○二○○號

http://www.sanmin.com.tw　三民網路書店